This book belongs to

For permission requests, please contact:
studio@raveenabaskaran.com

Published by:
Raveena Baskaran
ISBN (PB) : 978-93-344-3714-0
ISBN (HB) : 978-93-344-4004-1

Fishomania

Adult Coloring Book

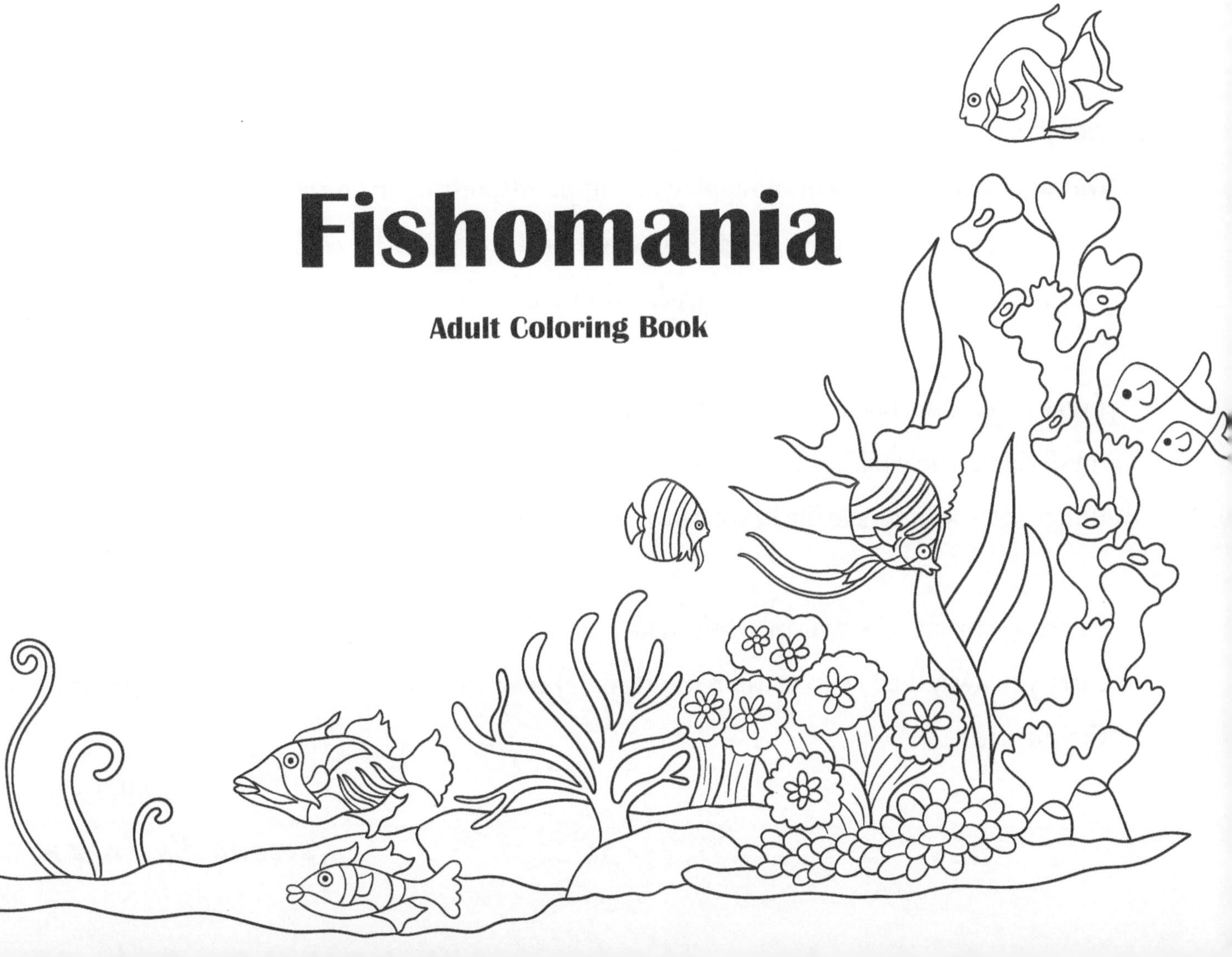

My Dear Creative Souls,

Are you ready to dive into a sea of creativity? In Fishomania, you'll explore an enchanting underwater world where graceful fishes swirl through coral gardens, shimmering bubbles, and flowing waves. Each page invites you to relax, color freely, and immerse yourself in the calm rhythm of aquatic life.

You'll discover a variety of fish species — from the tiniest guppies to majestic Whale — each surrounded by beautiful underwater elements. You might find them gliding through vast oceans, swimming playfully in ponds, resting in cozy fishbowls, or exploring lively aquariums. Some pages even feature delightful companions like turtles, jellyfish, seahorses, shells, and starfish, adding to the ocean's magical charm.

Every fish in this book can be anything you imagine — real or whimsical, bright or mysterious. The choice is entirely yours. Let your colors and creativity bring these underwater wonders to life in your own unique way.

So grab your favorite coloring tools, take a deep breath, and let the waves of creativity carry you away. Each stroke will remind you of the serenity and wonder hidden beneath the surface.

With Love,

Raveena Baskaran

To see adult coloring book-related videos, visit my YouTube channel:
https://www.youtube.com/@raveenabaskaran

Get the digital version of my coloring books here: https://store.raveenabaskaran.com/

My Amazon store:
https://www.amazon.com/stores/Raveena-Baskaran/author/B0CNH5SZK6

Your thoughts mean the world to me — if this book brought you joy, please take a moment to leave a review.

If you purchased the book on Amazon, consider leaving a review to help others discover the joy of coloring these beauty.

I highly value your thoughts and suggestions. Feel free to send your feedback and comments directly to my mail studio@raveenabaskaran.com.
Your insights can contribute to making future editions even better.

Follow me on social media **@coloring_raveena** for updates, exclusive content, and more creative inspiration. Let's stay connected and keep the artistic conversation going.

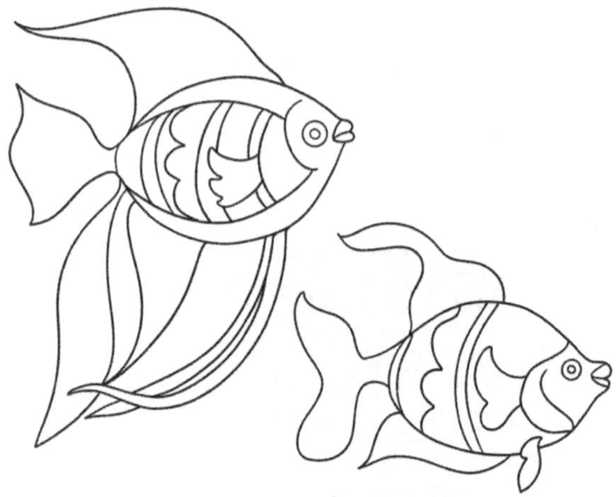

My Other Works:

Don't forget to check out the other books in the Mania series for more creative adventures!

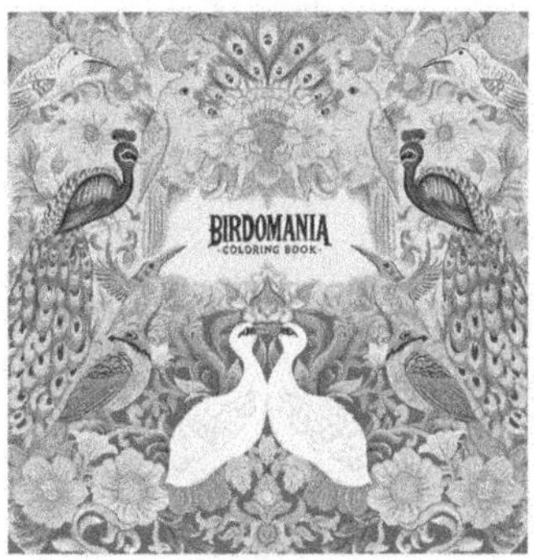

COLOR PALETTE EXPLORATION

COLOR PALETTE EXPLORATION

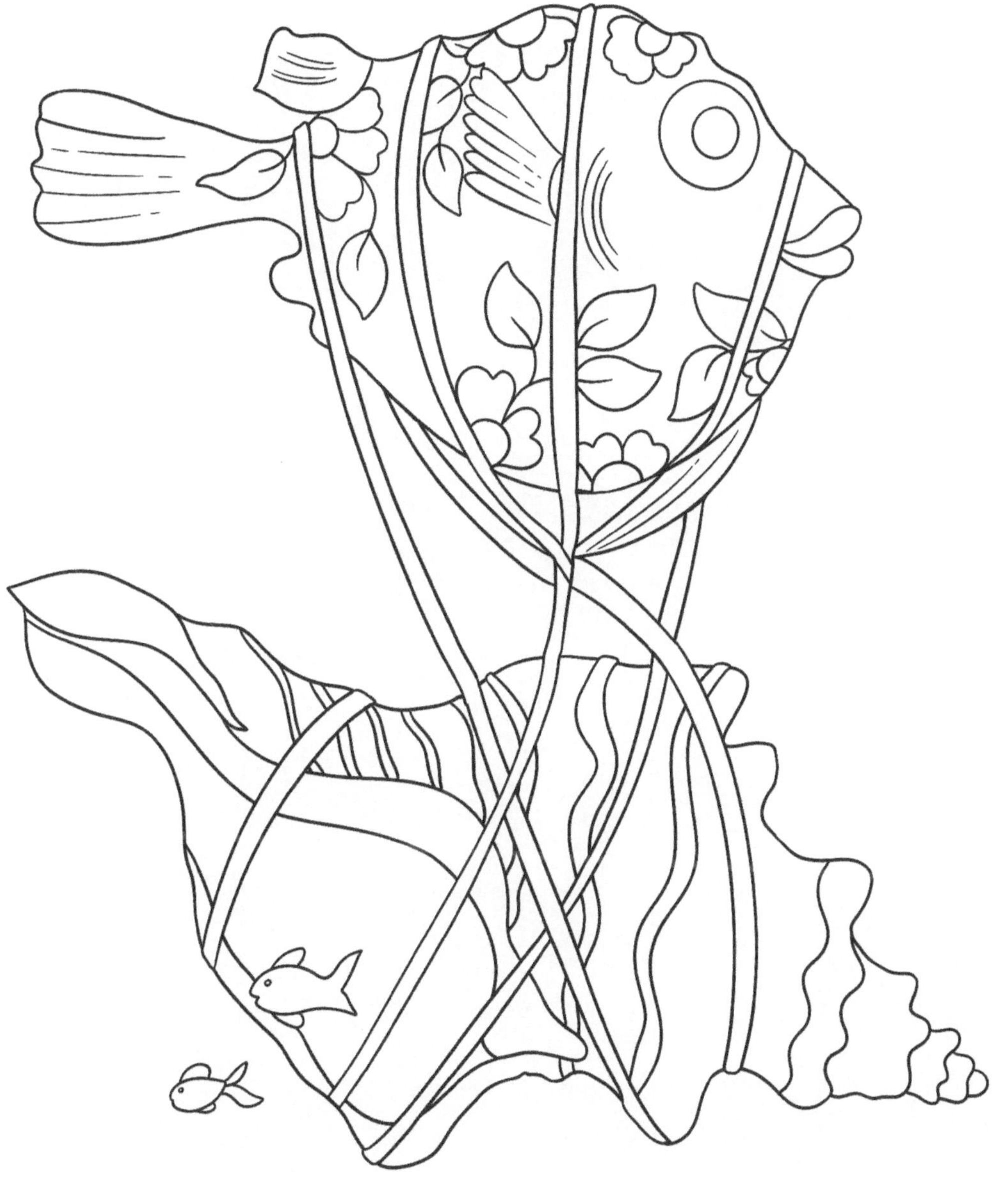

Printed at Repro India Ltd.